Forgiveness

Forgiveness

Dani DiPirro

WATKINS
Sharing Wisdom Since
1893

Forgiveness
Dani DiPirro

First published in the UK and USA in 2016
by Watkins, an imprint of Watkins
Media Limited
19 Cecil Court
London WC2N 4EZ

enquiries@watkinspublishing.co.uk

Copyright © Watkins Media Limited 2016
Text copyright © Dani DiPirro 2016
Artwork copyright © Dani DiPirro 2016

Development Editor: Kelly Thompson
Managing Editor: Fiona Robertson
Editor: Dawn Bates
Head of Design: Viki Ottewill
Design: Dani DiPirro
Production: Uzma Taj

A CIP record for this book is available
from the British Library

ISBN: 978-1-78028-949-6

10 9 8 7 6 5 4 3 2 1

Typeset in Gotham
Printed in China

www.watkinspublishing.com

To all those who have forgiven me and to those I have forgiven, I am forever grateful. Because of you, I was inspired to write this.

INTRODUCTION

Forgiveness is one of the most valuable skills you can master. Whether wrongs you have suffered are minor or a cause of great pain, releasing feelings of blame and putting the negative episodes behind you is both empowering and uplifting.

There's no doubt that forgiving can be a challenge if you have been hurt. It's natural to avoid things that have caused pain and all too easy to bear grudges. But when you forgive (even if you don't forget), you open up space in your heart and mind for love. And the more you love, the more you create a positive and mindful life for yourself.

This little book explores the meaning of forgiveness and its different manifestations. It has been designed to help you learn the art of forgiving others and also yourself, and, in doing so, set yourself free from the emotional burden of past pain.

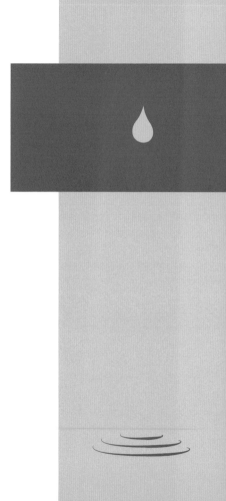

FORGIVENESS

noun | for•give•ness

1. The act of letting go of anger or blame toward another person

2. The attitude of being willing to forgive

In spite of everything,
I still believe that people
are really **good at heart**.

Anne Frank
German-born diarist (1929–1945)

If someone has hurt you, try not to judge the whole person on the basis of a single wrongdoing. Think of all the ways in which this person has enriched your life, so you do not focus on just one painful experience.

Name three good things about someone you want to forgive.

TODAY I **SEE GOODNESS** AND RELEASE BLAME.

He that cannot forgive others **breaks the bridge over which he must pass** himself; for every man has **need to be forgiven.**

Thomas Fuller
English churchman and historian (1608–1661)

PEACE

GENEROSITY

UNBURDENING

We all need forgiveness at times. By offering that generosity to others, we make it more likely our own mistakes will be forgiven. When we choose to let go of past wrongs, we give our heart and mind opportunities for more freedom and contentment – and we inspire others to forgive, too.

Ponder what it would feel like to receive forgiveness.

TODAY I FORGIVE TO SET MYSELF FREE.

**Forgiveness is a
virtue of the brave**.

Indira Gandhi
Indian stateswoman (1917–1984)

When we think of all the pain in the world, it becomes challenging to forgive those responsible. The next time you hear of someone causing suffering, recognize that they, too, have felt heartache, and their own pain may have led to their actions. Can you find the strength to forgive them?

Identify an act of pain and forgive the person or people who caused it.

TODAY I AM **STRONG ENOUGH** TO FORGIVE.

Forgiveness is the **key** to **action** and freedom.

Hannah Arendt
German-born political theorist (1906–1975)

If you cling closely to the wrongs done to you, they will come to define who you are and prevent you from being who you want to be. Note how much time you have wasted focusing on your hurt. Try talking it through with a friend or writing it down, then let it go and move forward.

Write down a hurtful episode and release it by throwing it away.

TODAY I
FORGIVE TO
LET MYSELF
MOVE ON.

One **forgives** to the degree that one **loves**.

François de La Rochefoucauld
French author (1613-1680)

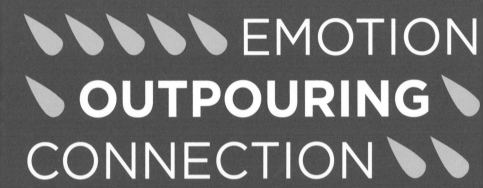

Love makes it easier to offer genuine forgiveness. At first, when someone you love wrongs you, the pain you feel can make it difficult to open your heart to forgiveness. But by rising above the pain and showing love, you ensure the bond between you is forged even stronger than before.

Reach out lovingly to someone you love who has hurt you.

TODAY I **OFFER LOVE** INSTEAD OF ANGER.

How unhappy is he who cannot **forgive himself**.

Publilius Syrus
Syrian-born Latin writer (1st century BC)

CARE
COMPASSION
POTENTIAL

Looking back all the time will not help you live the life you want. You cannot change what's been done, but you *can* influence how you act from now on. Make today – and future days – brighter by choosing to forgive yourself now for mistakes you've made in the past.

Think of a past bad choice and consider what you have learned from it.

TODAY I FORGIVE MYSELF FOR MY PAST MISTAKES.

Don't spend **time** beating on a wall, hoping to **transform** it into a door.

Coco Chanel
French fashion designer (1883–1971)

It's important to remember that mistakes sometimes simply happen. Forgiveness involves accepting that some situations and people may never change, and choosing to embrace those situations and love those people in spite of their flaws.

Try to accept others as they are, with all their weaknesses.

TODAY I FORGIVE
THE FLAWS
IN OTHERS.

Forgiveness is the fragrance that the violet sheds on the heel that has crushed it.

Mark Twain
American author (1835–1910)

There is real beauty in cultivating forgiveness. It might seem a small thing to let go of resentment, but this has a big impact on the world around us. Our positive attitude rubs off on the people we forgive and stays with them, encouraging them to be forgiving to others in turn.

Do one wonderful thing for someone you forgive.

TODAY I FORGIVE AND **CREATE BEAUTY.**

Pain is **never permanent**.

Saint Teresa of Ávila
Spanish mystic and author (1515–1582)

Giving yourself time to experience pain when you've been hurt is part of the process of forgiveness. But no pain can last for ever. However upset you are, be patient and leave a space for forgiveness to grow. Time can be an amazing healer that helps hurts and grudges fade away.

Reach out to someone and rebuild bridges.

TODAY I
**EMBRACE
THE POWER
OF TIME
TO HEAL.**

Always forgive **your enemies**; nothing annoys them so much.

Oscar Wilde
Irish author (1854–1900)

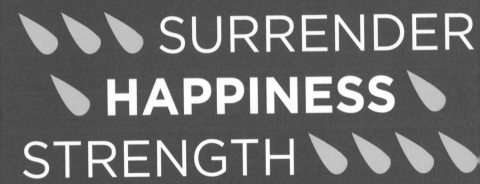

A humorous attitude to your "enemies" will help you untie yourself emotionally from them. Can you let go of grudges and accept other people's rights to their opinions, even if you don't agree with them? If you can do this, you'll be in a happier emotional state.

Imagine any resentment you have simply floating away.

TODAY I FORGIVE ALL THOSE WHO HAVE HURT ME.

The ineffable joy of forgiving and being forgiven forms an ecstasy that might well arouse the envy of the gods.

Elbert Hubbard
American philosopher and author (1856–1915)

RELIEF
FREEDOM
EXHILARATION

Forgiving and being forgiven are experiences that remind us we are all human, prone to making mistakes and united by strong bonds of love that make us want to forgive again and again. Sometimes it's the most difficult acts of forgiveness that are the most uplifting and life-affirming.

Think of the last time you forgave. What positive emotions arose from that?

TODAY I FORGIVE AND **FEEL POSITIVE EMOTIONS.**

" Forgiveness is the **economy of the heart** . . . forgiveness **saves the expense** of anger, the cost of hatred, the waste of spirits. **"**

Hannah More
English philanthropist and author (1745–1833)

Holding onto anger takes a lot of time and energy that could be used in so many more positive ways. There are countless benefits to a calm, forgiving approach to life that focuses on love and kindness instead of anger and resentment.

Inspire someone to forgive by sharing how you have moved on.

TODAY I LET GO
OF ANGER TO
**MAKE SPACE
FOR GOOD.**

Before we can **forgive** one another, we have to **understand** one another.

Emma Goldman
Russian-born anarchist and author (1869–1940)

You may be able to forgive sooner if you can try to talk honestly with – and listen calmly to – the person you feel has wronged you. There are usually reasons for someone's actions. Taking time to understand their motivations will likely lead to compassion and, in turn, to forgiveness.

Ask someone you want to forgive how they feel.

TODAY I FORGIVE _____ BY **TRYING TO UNDERSTAND**.

Forgiveness is the **giving**, and so the receiving, of **life**.

George MacDonald
Scottish author and minister (1824-1905)

Forgiveness has a positive impact on the lives of the people you forgive, freeing them of the heaviness that worry and guilt can create. And these acts of forgiveness will also help *you*, giving you more time and energy to appreciate each moment.

Write about a time you chose forgiveness over anger and what it taught you.

TODAY I **SEE JOY** IN FORGIVING OTHERS.

"

It does not matter
how **slowly** you go as
long as you **do not stop**.

Confucius
Chinese philosopher (551–479 BC)

STEADINESS
GENTLENESS
SELF-LOVE

It is good to forgive ourselves when life becomes challenging and we feel like we're failing to reach our goals. Sometimes just staying in the same place is a victory in itself. Accept that we all move at a different pace, depending on circumstances.

Can you take one small step toward a goal that's important to you?

TODAY I **RECOGNIZE WITH LOVE** ALL MY EFFORTS.

Let us forgive each other - only then will we live in peace.

Leo Tolstoy
Russian author (1828–1910)

It is all too easy to hold onto, perhaps even relish, our grudges; our dislikes can, at times, be a way of bonding with others. But if we feed resentment in this way, it will eat away at us from the inside. You will feel more at peace if you release corrosive or otherwise negative emotions.

Replace conversations about a grudge with more positive topics.

TODAY I FIND PEACE IN WHAT I SAY.

Someone has to die in order that the rest of us should **value life** more.

Virginia Woolf
English author (1882–1941)

When someone very dear to you dies or moves on from your relationship, it's natural to feel betrayed or angry. Forgive those who are no longer in your life, whatever pain they caused in the leaving of it. Such losses can help you appreciate relationships you're still lucky to have – and life itself.

Offer loving kindness to someone no longer with you.

TODAY I
APPRECIATE
**THOSE I
HAVE LOST.**

There isn't time . . . for bickerings, apologies, heartburnings, callings to account. There is only time for **loving**.

Mark Twain
American author (1835–1910)

Each of us has only a short time on this planet. Do we really want to waste it on petty resentments? Our experiences are shaped by our perceptions, so we need only become more mindful of positive experiences for our lives to seem richer, more loving and more full of joy.

Thank someone who has made your life better.

TODAY I LET IN
FORGIVENESS
BY **BEING
GRATEFUL.**

TOP 10 WAYS TO LIVE A LIFE OF FORGIVENESS

1. Recognize we all make mistakes

2. Avoid judging harshly

3. Accept that we're all different

4. Make an effort to understand

5. Don't cling to resentment

6. Love people (faults and all)

7. Act with compassion

8. Don't stay stuck in the past

9. Focus on the good, not the bad

10. Be ready to move forward freely

TOP 10 WAYS TO BE FORGIVING AT HOME

1. Allow for imperfections

2. Don't look for reasons to be angry

3. Seek out the positive

4. Be willing to apologize

5. Accept apologies graciously

6. Speak from a place of gentleness

7. Don't dwell on small disagreements

8. Be grateful for what you have

9. Recognize the effects of stress

10. See the value of love over resentment

TOP 10 WAYS TO BE FORGIVING TO YOURSELF

1. Accept that you're only human

2. Don't dwell on your mistakes

3. But do learn from past errors

4. Apologize to anyone you've hurt

5. Focus on your best traits

6. Don't put pressure on yourself

7. Accept your body as it is

8. Allow yourself to feel how you feel

9. Trust you're doing the best you can

10. Let go of guilt and move forward

TOP 10 WAYS TO BE FORGIVING AT WORK

1. Don't obsess over petty mishaps

2. Avoid letting issues fester

3. Make an effort to resolve conflict

4. Express how you feel and move on

5. Notice good qualities in others

6. Ask "why?" when you don't know

7. Be as empathetic as possible

8. Speak and act with kindness

9. Accept that mistakes happen

10. Help others learn from their mistakes

TOP 10 WAYS TO BE FORGIVING IN LOVE

1. Be open to hearing "I'm sorry"

2. Strive to be empathetic

3. Take time to heal your own pain

4. Shift from blame to understanding

5. Acknowledge the suffering of others

6. Speak with loving kindness

7. Remember happy times

8. Get support from your friends

9. Recall a time you were forgiven

10. Choose to let go of the pain

NOTE TO READER

Hello! I'm Dani. I hope you've enjoyed reading this little book as much as I enjoyed creating it. Forgiveness, I've learned, is an essential part of living a meaningful, fulfilled and peaceful life.

In 2009 I created **PositivelyPresent.com**. Since setting up that website, I've gone on to write multiple ebooks and publish *The Positively Present Guide to Life*, as well as design diaries for Watkins' *Every Day Matters* series. I also work as a graphic designer. In work and in life,

I've had my ups and downs. As a result, I've learned a great deal about forgiveness and how important it can be to moving on and finding a happier way of being. I hope this book helps you to forgive and be forgiven.

If you want to learn more about me or my work, check out **DaniDiPirro.com**, or visit **PositivelyPresent.com** for inspiration on living positively in the present.